If God Used Sticky Notes®

for Friends

From: God
To: All

Keep these
in your heart!
love,
God

Illustrations and text by

Chris Shea

HARVEST HOUSE PUBLISHERS

If God Used Sticky Notes® for Friends

Published by Harvest House Publishers
Eugene, Oregon 97402
www.harvesthousepublishers.com

ISBN-13: 978-0-7369-2186-2
ISBN-10: 0-7369-2186-9

Design and production by Garborg Design Works, Savage, Minnesota

Scripture quotations are taken from the King James Version of the Bible.

Printed in China

08 09 10 11 12 13 14 15 / LP / 10 9 8 7 6 5 4 3 2 1

For Roberta...

"Hi, Love! God is good!"

With gratitude for your words that stick with me today.

I'll be seeing you...

CS

I wonder where I'd find them,
and I wonder what they'd say

if I asked God to send
a few sticky notes
to help me tell you how glad I am
we're friends today.

Maybe on the refrigerator
beside a photo of us at the beach

How much fun
could the ocean
be
all by yourself?
Love, God

And the gathering of the
waters called he Seas.
Genesis 1:10

or on my calendar where your
birthday is circled in red

I create only
the best, don't
you think?
XºG.

And God saw everything that
he had made, and, behold, it
was very good.
Genesis 1:31

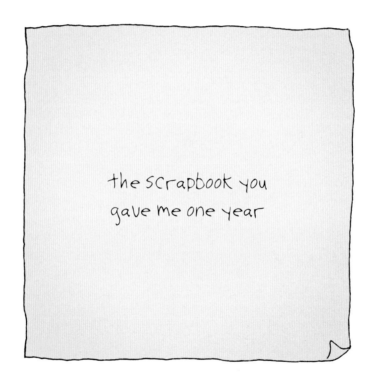

the scrapbook you
gave me one year

MY HAPPY DAYS

True friends are a treasure to keep forever!
Love, God

The memory of the just is blessed.

Proverbs 10:7

my kitchen table

14

Isn't it just amazing
how much love a
coffee cake holds?
Love, God

He that is of a merry heart
hath a continual feast.
Proverbs 15:15

the backyard fence

my telephone

or the shopping bags hanging
on the back of the door.

What if every hour of the day
everyone found them,
little notes of love put here
for each of us,

23

reminding us that God is real
and that He cares about us
enough to give us friends to
go through life with?

A pink one on the garden hose
that always seems to drip

Pretty flowers!
Thoughtful words!
The perfect surprise gift!
love,
God.

The words of a man's mouth
are as deep waters.

Proverbs 18:4

a blue one on the
mailbox post
where geraniums
and ivy bloom

I think you got a
letter from your
friend today!
                XO God

A man that hath friends
must show himself
friendly.
          Proverbs 18:24

29

a yellow one on the
cafe table
where we meet our
friends for tea

Isn't it great having someone who'll keep your secrets? (Besides me!)
xoxo God

A word fitly spoken is like apples of gold.
Proverbs 25:11

or a lavender one on
the comforter,
the last thing we read before
we go to sleep at night.

Say your prayers!
Count your blessings!
Bless your friends!

Love,
God

Every word of God
is pure.
Proverbs 30:5

When we really look for them
we can see that sticky notes from
God are everywhere,
little reminders of how present He is
in everything we do.

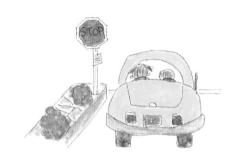

35

Because God is always able to catch our eye

through the kindness of
a new friend

or the thoughtfulness of one
we have cherished forever.

Dear You...
How many
years has it
been ??
Happy Birthday
with love xo

41

Because daily God surrounds us
with friends like you,
made in His image,
friends who fill our lives
with steadfast love and loyalty
reflecting His great good heart.

43

A newspaper carried to
the front door
and left there with a card

45

laughter brightening
an afternoon
through a silly story
from a friend

47

the comfort of a hug
when tears just won't stop falling

the way a homemade cookie
tastes when it comes from
the kitchen of a friend

each a kind of sticky note God
provides us day and night
all the days of our lives

because He wants to keep
in touch with us and remind us of
the beauty of our ordinary days.

I know that if I found them,
sticky notes from God
that helped me tell you
"thank you"
for all you mean to me,

they would decorate every
place we've ever been,
every place we've ever
sat and talked
and shared the secrets
of our hearts.

There would be so many of them
so filled with sweet reminders
of just how much He must love me

because, that He loves me
could be the only reason
there is for finding
a friend like you.

63

I bless the path that brought us together.
You are everything a friend could be.

My cup runneth over.
Psalm 23:5